*"I get asked to review a lot of h
ally left embarrassed trying to j
not the case with this book. It's
has put into it are evident from ... page, and you're never far
away from a nice chuckle. I'm not usually a Harhur, but I thoroughly
commend and recommend this excellent book."*

– **Andy Kind, comedy writer**

*"If you've ever wondered whether it is possible to make the Bible
mean what it never meant... wonder no more! But if you invest
some 'Minniths', you'll discover things about 'Heman' that may have
more to do with 'Caesar' than your getting the 'Gaash' treatment
(now you'll need to buy the book!).*

*"And if you die laughing, they'll give you your money back (upon
personal application!)"*

– **Steve Brady, Principal, Moorlands College**

"Nigel Bayley makes me laugh and if you read this book you'll see why.

*"When we laugh our defences come down and we can learn...
which may make this a learning book as well as a laughing one."*

– **Ian Coffey, author and speaker**

*"This book is wonderfully irreverent, uncomfortably hilarious and
joyfully provocative. Read it. Laugh out loud. And think before you
speak from now on..."*

– **Matt Summerfield, Executive Director, Urban Saints**

The Most Unreliable Bible Dictionary, Ever!

Words You Never Knew You Needed

Nigel Bayley

MONARCH
BOOKS
Oxford, UK & Grand Rapids, Michigan, USA

Text copyright © 2013 Nigel Bayley
This edition copyright © 2013 Lion Hudson

The right of Nigel Bayley to be identified as the author of this work has been asserted by him in accordance with the Copyright, Designs and Patents Act 1988.

All rights reserved. No part of this publication may be reproduced or transmitted in any form or by any means, electronic or mechanical, including photocopy, recording, or any information storage and retrieval system, without permission in writing from the publisher.

Published by Monarch Books
an imprint of
Lion Hudson plc
Wilkinson House, Jordan Hill Road,
Oxford OX2 8DR, England
Email: monarch@lionhudson.com
www.lionhudson.com/monarch

ISBN 978 0 85721 508 6
e-ISBN 978 0 85721 509 3

First edition 2013

Illustrations by Bridget Gillespie

A catalogue record for this book is available from the British Library

Printed and bound in Malta, August 2013, LH28

Acknowledgments

Elaine, who God has rather wonderfully allowed me to share life with. Thanks for everything you are and everything you do. You're the only one for me.

Hannah and Josh, for putting up with my terrible jokes and sometimes even laughing. You're both brill and I'm very proud to be your Dad.

All those at Lymington Baptist Church, who still seem to like me after nearly nine years. Oh, and any resemblance any of you might have to people in this book is entirely coincidental.

My Mum, who bore me (apparently) and whose support is unfailing.

To Gary, John, and Ben, for saying the stuff that I don't want to hear but desperately need to. And for being the best friends I've ever had.

Thanks also to all of those who have helped me bring this book to life:

John Arthur, for helping me see the vision of this book more clearly while letting it remain wholly mine. And for writing some of the more unruly definitions that reside within it, including that one which doesn't. Sorry, I just couldn't.

Andy Kind, a proper comedian and author who became a friend, who really believed in me despite plenty of evidence to the contrary, and then helped me to find some more people who did too.

Dave Gooderidge, a good boss and a better friend, for being my primary source of feedback, often whether I like it or not, but in this case in generous response to my request. And for Barabbas.

Michael Walsh, for reading through and correcting mistakes while serving up the usual side dish of encouragement.

And special thanks to those at Lion Hudson:

Tony Collins, for giving this chancer a chance.

Jenny Ward, Miranda Lever, and everyone else who has worked hard to make me look good.

And believe me, that is hard work – just ask Elaine.

But most of all, to him who is able to keep me from stumbling and to present me before his glorious presence without fault and with great joy – to the only God our Saviour be glory, majesty, power and authority, through Jesus Christ our Lord, before all ages, now and for evermore! So be it.

Introduction

So there was this dictionary in the 1980s called *The Meaning of Liff*.

> **Liff (n.)** A common object or experience for which no word yet exists.

Douglas Adams and John Lloyd used place names as words for these liffs and it was splendidly funny.

And I loved it.

And then one day, many years later, it suddenly dawned on me that someone should write a Christian dictionary along the same lines.

Because, having had a lifetime of adventures in churches, I was acutely aware that in church life there are countless objects and experiences that we know only too well, but for which no words yet exist.

And that there are countless wonderful words in the Bible, magnificent names of places and people, that need a fresh opportunity to be enjoyed by all.

And then later that same day, it suddenly dawned on me that I have had a lifetime of adventures in churches and that the someone should probably be me.

So here it is.

And why, exactly?

Good question.

I love the church. It's not yet all it could be. But I love it.

I really liked *The Sacred Diary of Adrian Plass*, because there were absurdities in churches that I didn't think anyone was allowed to talk about. And then he did. And although I wasn't quite sure if that was OK, I was absolutely certain that it was hilarious.

And I don't think we laugh enough – especially not at ourselves.

And sometimes when we laugh at ourselves, we see the absurdities in us.

And I think that's a good thing.

Maybe you don't.

If you don't, you should probably put this book down, glance around to check that no one saw you looking at it, and quickly pick up a proper Christian book. There are loads of brilliant ones.

Otherwise, I think you're probably ready to laugh.

If so, this book is for you. I hope you enjoy it.

Nigel Bayley
@babydrums

If you have any unreliable comments, or wish to send in your own unreliable definitions, please use any of the following:
@mostunreliable
www.facebook.com/mostunreliable
mostunreliable@gmail.com

Note: Terms in italics are given their definitions elsewhere in this dictionary.

Abaddon (adj.)
Descriptive of the new minister as they begin to try to make changes.

Abdi (v.)
To neatly sidestep responsibility for your repeated sinful behaviour by announcing: "That's just the way I am."

Abel (n.)
One who has the opportunity to pray for someone to be healed but decides not to do so in case it doesn't work and they make God look bad.

Abel Maim (n.)
An *abel* whose prayers not asking for healing are entirely effective.

Abishag (n.)
The despairing look that quickly follows on from a *terah* when the only response that eventually comes is the sound of two *bezers* arguing about what the nice man at the front is asking.

Achaicus (n.)
One who believeth that none but the Authorised Version is given by inspiration of God.

Achish (n.)
The sneeze of a baby during a critical point of ministry that makes everyone go "aww" and rather spoils the moment.

Addon (n.)
The thirty-*minnith* period following the obvious closing point of the sermon, during which the preacher, for some reason known only to themselves, is still preaching.

Adin (n.)
That which the youth band makes.

Adoraim (n.)
One who cleverly uses the phrase "in love" as permission to unleash a tirade of abuse at someone.

Agag (n.)
An unintentional pun made by the preacher, which gets considerably more laughs than their carefully prepared jokes, and as a result has just managed to hijack the most profound part of the message.

Agrippa (n.)
A look of calm serenity on the face of the minister, despite the utter mayhem going on all around. This is what a minister needs to quickly find after a *kadesh barnea* and is why you will sometimes hear people saying, "He needs to get agrippa himself".

Ahikam (n.)
A filming device positioned in the balcony for the purpose of recording a christening or baptism.

Ahira (n.)
An elderly individual who loves nothing more than hearing the young people getting involved in church, but just wonders if they could be turned down a little.

Ahuzzath (n.)
That moment, a short while after the *uzzah*, at which the undignified dancing breaks out and the *sadducees* leave.

Ai (n.)
The involuntary outburst of a *colossae* who has been *tishbiting* and finally gets to the table, only to discover that all the food has gone except for seven cherry tomatoes, a handful of peanuts, a small slice of soggy vegetarian quiche, and a mountain of lettuce.

Aiah (n.)
A greeting you hear every few seconds if you employ a teenager as a welcomer.

Akbor (n.)
The moment during a sermon when your head suddenly lolls forward and you realize that today's message is not quite as impactful as you had hoped it would be. This is particularly embarrassing if you are the preacher.

THE MOST UNRELIABLE BIBLE DICTIONARY, EVER!

Akbor

"I think we must have missed the all-night vigil again, dear."

Amaziah (n.)
One who complains about the worship in a way that makes it appear they believe that it was meant to be for their benefit.

Amok (n.)
A lively young child who always volunteers during a children's talk but is never chosen by anyone who knows them. As a visiting preacher, you know you have found an amok when you hear the communal intake of breath from the congregation.

Amorite (n.)
An alternative answer to "fine" for non-*sharezers*.

Anem (n.)
That which a *beeri* calls out rather too loudly at the end of the minister's opening prayer.

Ararat (n.)
That which a *dishan* shouts upon spotting a rodent in the kitchen. This is often followed by a word no one has ever heard her utter before.

Arimathea (n.)
One who counts the offering. Often also a button collector.

Armageddon (n.)
The inevitable upcoming dreadful day when *sodom and gomorrah* will be in the same Sunday School group.

Arumah (n.)
One who seems to know everything about everyone but annoyingly refuses to tell anyone any of it for fear of being thought a *lo-ruhamah*.

Attai (n.)
The unspoken yet essential Sunday morning dress code for retired churchgoing gentlemen.

Azbuk (n.)
One who refuses to sing the words from the screen, preferring to stick with their ancient copy of "Mission Praise 2".

Baal (v.)
That which the babies always seem to do when you're on crèche duty.

Baal Gad (n.)
A step on from *gadding*, a baal gad is a technical move whereby you actually pick up coins from inside the receptacle, and then throw them back down into it in order to make a suitably generous sounding noise. Alternatively, if there is a bank note in there, you can just loudly rustle that.

Baal Meon (n.)
A *baalah* who manages to be so precisely out of tune that they cause those around them to have absolutely no idea at any given moment what note it is they are supposed to be singing.

Baal Zephon (n.)
A feeling of extreme embarrassment that replaces a *zephon* the moment it dawns on you that the ringing mobile phone is in fact yours.

Baalah (n.)
One who has no idea of the tune of the chosen hymn so just sings the words loudly.

Baanah (n.)
An impromptu prayer meeting which has ballooned out of all control because none of those present have any idea which of them has the authority to produce a *nimrah*.

Babylon (n.)
A sudden desire to help in the crèche that coincidentally overwhelms you in the aftermath of an *ogging*.

Bakbuk (n.)
That knackered old lectern Bible that has been taking up valuable space in a cupboard for ten years because people are genuinely worried that throwing God's Word away could be the unforgivable sin.

Bamah (n.)
The now massively increased volume of the drummer following the construction of a large Perspex screen which gives them the freedom to play five times louder than they ever did before.

Barabbas (n.)
The recently closed weekly meeting which currently has a group of people campaigning for its reinstatement, despite the fact that none of the group were ever seen at it when it was running.

Bathsheba (n.)
A makeshift baptistry.

Beeri (n.)
One who attends the Christmas Eve midnight service in a jolly mood having previously attended a number of other establishments.

Beno (n.)
A praying posture based on the aircraft crash position, which is carefully designed to show off your humility.

Beri (v.)
To decline to admit that you've *zivved* when the individual concerned comes and thanks you profusely for your prayers, describing in great detail the enormous difference they made.

Besor (n.)
A church that finally takes the plunge and has the antique uncomfortable pews removed, only to then replace them with brand new uncomfortable pews.

Beth Dagon (n.)
The moment during a sermon when you actually stopped listening. Generally, this is approximately six minutes (or around seventeen *minniths*) earlier than a *dagon*.

Beth Nimrah (n.)
One who has failed with such regularity to successfully end prayer meetings with a *nimrah*, they now start every final prayer with "So, Lord" and end it with "Please be with us as we go out from here", just to be sure.

Beth Peor (n.)
A female *peor*. Beth peors only ever leave the sermon in pairs.

Betonim (n.)
An attempt to chalk up a prostrate and clearly unwell old man as the result of a dramatic move of the Holy Spirit and therefore a good starter for ten on the long-awaited revival.

Bezer (n.)
An elderly individual who appears to be entirely unaware that their hearing aid is feeding back and deafening everyone around them.

Blastus (n.)
The look of hungry intent from a congregation that hopes the visiting preacher might probe the theological depth that seriously eludes the lightweight currently occupying the vicarage.

Bokim (n.)
One who prays out loud immediately after the minister has called for a time of silence.

Bul (n.)
A "truth" that clearly cannot be found in today's passage, but which the preacher has elected to bring out of it anyway.

Buzi (adj.)
That which everyone suddenly becomes when the minister is seeking a babysitter for *sodom and gomorrah*.

Byblos (n.)
The belief shared by many that while the Word of God is definitely sharper than any double-edged sword, it can only in fact penetrate the first five rows of seats. But avoid the sixth too just in case.

C

Caesar (v.)
What everyone thinks the strict churches do to a woman who isn't wearing a hat.

Cain (v.)
To ask someone if it's their first time at your church, only to discover that they've been going longer than you.

Carchemish (adj.)
The super-spiritual way you feel when someone says "Yes, Lord" during one of your prayers.

Castor and Pollux (ns.)
The large gentlemen who always get called upon when the piano needs moving.

Chuza (n.)
The moment you realize that you have started singing the song an octave too high and need to quickly decide whether to suddenly switch down, or risk trying to hit notes you haven't been close to since you were nine.

THE MOST UNRELIABLE BIBLE DICTIONARY, EVER!

Chuza

"Stop that Norman, you know it sets the dogs off!"

Clement (adj.)
Descriptive of the beautiful weather you get on a church outing that suddenly convinces everyone that there really must be a God after all, and causes *gideons* to come close to spontaneously combusting.

Colossae (n.)
One who has a 100 per cent attendance record at events that provide food.

Cretans (pl. n.)
Those who are demanding to know why the worship isn't like that which they just experienced at Spring Harvest, apparently unaware that your music band currently consists of two rhythmically challenged tambourinists, a tone-deaf octogenarian pianist, and a woman with two-thirds of a flute.

Crispus (n.)
The need for some individuals to have been "dangled over the pit of hell" in order for them to feel they have been properly preached to.

Cush (v.)
To pretend to take notes on your smartphone during an evening meeting while actually checking the football scores.

Cushi (adj.)
Pertaining to the easy job at the friendly little church that all the other ministers seem to get.

D

Dagon (n.)
The moment during a sermon at which you suddenly realize you are no longer listening.

Dalmatia (n.)
Where some of the *kenites* come from.

Darkon (n.)
The crippling temptation to shriek, "Help!", and then use the ensuing confusion to escape from a sermon which has, by its length alone, already made you want to set fire to the preacher's trousers.

Dedan (n.)
Anyone who tells a *sadducee* to cheer up.

Desert of Zin (n.)
That awkward period of time when the worship leader appears to be leading a completely different song than the one that is currently being projected onto the screen.

Deuel (n.)
Any discussion on church policy which includes the church secretary and the minister.

Diblaim (adj.)
Not present at a church meeting and therefore liable to have someone *pinon* you. As issues are raised, people will ask "Who is diblaim?"

Dibon Gad (n.)
A dibon gad is the ultimate expression of *gadding* and requires you to put on your most embarrassed expression and glance humbly around the room, nodding gently in appreciation, as people applaud the announcement of a large financial gift that was given anonymously.

Dishan (n.)
A lady who is always busily working in the church kitchen, even when there appears to be absolutely nothing to do in there.

Dodo (n.)
One who forgets to turn their clock back and arrives at church an hour late. This does not include those who have done it deliberately in order to arrive just in time for coffee.

Dor (n.)
That which a minister would love to show to a *pekah*.

Dorcas (n.)
One who prays after a *nimrah* causing all those who had already looked up to quickly get back into a *beno*.

Edom (n.)
A small boy who is considerably louder than everybody else during the annual rendition of "Away in a Manger". This would be bearable were it not for the added fact that he is considerably less tuneful than everybody else.

Eldaah (n.)
An individual of advanced years who loudly inquires as to what's going on and thereby beautifully violates the holy moment the minister has just carefully engendered.

Eli (n.)
(Rare) One who has never fallen asleep during a prayer meeting.

Eltekon (n.)
A *tekelling* that went so appallingly badly that your packet of sweets is currently two rows in front and is still being passed from one "generous" person to another.

Esau (n.)
One who regularly shares at "Bring and Share" lunches but has never been known to do any bringing.

Eutychus (n.)
One who has fallen profoundly, and audibly, asleep in the middle of a meeting. Eventually the individual concerned will wake up with a start and all parties will then behave as if it simply never happened.

Felix (n.)
The not altogether disagreeable sensation, upon ruminating over a rather thoughtful and well-delivered sermon, that something will have to change, which grows to become spectacularly unpleasant the more you fail to shake it off.

Festus (adj.)
The smell of the church during Harvest.

Fortunatus (n.)
The ancient sect of believers who, during a prayer meeting, despite all instruction and exhortation to the contrary, can only give exceedingly long prayers of a thanksgiving nature.

THE MOST UNRELIABLE BIBLE DICTIONARY, EVER!

Festus

"I just don't think that's what Reverend Joyce meant by 'Feedback'!"

Gaash (v.)
To use "I'll pray about it" to mean "no" when someone asks you to do something for the church.

Gad (v.)
To pretend to put money into the offering because you don't have any on you and you don't want people to think you're a *mizar*.

Gadarenes (pl. n.)
The archenemies of *gadders*, gadarenes are those who place extremely large bank notes carefully into the offering such that they stick out prominently and are visible to as many people as possible.

Gaius (n.)
An elderly individual who only knows the old-fashioned meanings to words and as a result is a continuous source of embarrassment to any happy young men.

THE MOST UNRELIABLE BIBLE DICTIONARY, EVER!

Gad

Garmite (n.)
A minister who people either love or hate. So basically all ministers (apart from those who are universally hated).

Gath Hepher (n.)
An elderly group member who tells the *hepher* the reference but manages to get it wrong, which confuses everybody and initiates two minutes of people saying different numbers to each other at gradually increasing volume.

Geber (n.)
The vague disquiet that it is taking twice the time, and three times the passion, to discuss the most suitable model of new vacuum cleaner for the church as it did to agree the overseas mission budget.

Geder (n.)
A single man who, during times of prayer ministry, always seems to believe that God is calling him to lay hands on the most attractive female in the room.

Gerasenes (pl. n.)
Those parts of movies that make a superb theological point, but which you can never show because they contain naughty words, naughty behaviour or, well, naughty bits.

Gether (n.)
That which *nergals* would persistently, and somewhat annoyingly, like the Lord to bind us to.

Gezer (n.)
A teenager who is utterly unaware of the concept of reverence, and who therefore unwittingly offends *urbanus* individuals by cheerfully describing God as both "phat" and "sick".

Gideon (n.)
One who gets enormously excited about the tiniest things by concluding that anything in life that goes slightly in their favour is a magnificent miracle of the Lord.

Gittites (pl. n.)
Those who constantly talk about how great the church up the road is, but never go there. Or even better for everyone else, move there.

Gob (n.)
The annoyingly verbose child in Sunday School who, when you deliver the classic "Come and lead if you think you can do a better job than me", proceeds to the front and does precisely that.

Gog (v.)
To drink from a glass of extremely odd-tasting Communion "wine" and then try to stop yourself working out what it was in order to think about what you should be thinking about.

Goshen (n.)
One who seems to enjoy confessing their sins in the most inappropriate way to the most inappropriate people at the most inappropriate time and in the most inappropriate settings.

Gudgodah (n.)
One who continually repeats a particular title for God when they pray, for example "Father, we thank you Father, that you are our father, Father." It is about halfway through listening to one of these prayers that you suddenly realize you are counting.

Guni (n.)
A sermon point that works beautifully but has a completely extraneous heading in order to ensure alliteration across all three points.

Gur Baal (n.)
A feeling that follows closely on from a *baal zephon* and consists of deep regret and shame, not because you've interrupted the service, but because everyone now knows you have "Shine Jesus, Shine" as your ringtone.

H

Habakkuk (n.)
The theological belief that someone with a better Christian life will have a larger mansion in heaven. This is extensively spoken of even though it is entirely impossible to find any reference to it in the Bible.

Habazziniah (n.)
The member of the choir who is slightly out of tune but can somehow never quite be located.

Hadoram (n.)
The final piece of the flooring that sits over the baptistry, which won't drop into place until it is jumped up and down upon by a stout gentleman. Or a bonny lady.

Haggai (n.)
(Archaic) One who is blissfully unaware that they have put the acetate on the overhead projector the wrong way round.

THE MOST UNRELIABLE BIBLE DICTIONARY, EVER!

Habakkuk

"Something tells me Mr Gardiner's mother didn't like your quip about a 'Tomb with a view'!"

Haggite (n.)
The delicate little angel who must be protected from the brutal crèche and so is kept in church to share with everyone the delights of endless whinging.

Hallelujah (n.)
A word fervently expressed immediately after the long-awaited conclusion of an *addon*.

Ham (adj.)
Descriptive of the standard of acting to which the church drama group aspires.

Hamonah (n.)
A vaguely belligerent woman who appears every year at the "Carols by Candlelight", yet still seems to be on a personal crusade to point out to anyone who will listen that this service is done very much better by the church up the road.

Hannathon (n.)
A *mushi* that goes on for so long that the hand-holding has now become acutely embarrassing for everyone except *jezebels*.

Harhur (n.)
(Rare) One who laughs at the minister's jokes.

Harim (n.)
The collective term for a group of young females gathered around a male worship leader.

Hasadiah (n.)
An appallingly poor quality homemade banner that has been attached to the wall and as a result of grace can now never be removed.

Hatita (n.)
A *hermogene* who is so certain of what God is going to do next that they offer to eat their hat if he doesn't.

Havilah (n.)
The ability to continue to make *moses* at exactly the right moments, even though you ceased listening to the prayer a long time previously.

Hazaiah (n.)
A flash of sublime theological revelation of earth-shattering significance that cannot now be remembered since it was interrupted by a lengthy phone call about the flower rota.

Hazzelelponi (n.)
The reason given by the small child in the crèche for her carefully orchestrated *kibroth hattaavah*. She has suddenly decided she cannot live without the small plastic toy that is the only thing that is currently able to keep her baby sister from *baaling* the place down.

Hebrews (pl. n.)
Some apparently hilarious joke about men and teabags.

Helam (v.)
That which you have been praying for God to do to someone for years, that he finally and rather frustratingly seems to have decided to do after a short and frankly substandard prayer from someone who has just started coming to church and "fancied having a go".

Heldai (n.)
The more widely used name for the Family Fun Day.

Helek (n.)
The strange amalgamation of words you end up saying when you realize you are swearing out loud in church and quickly try to cover it up. Unfortunately this usually only succeeds in making it even more obvious.

Heman (n.)
A red-blooded male who simply doesn't have a feminine side to get in touch with, and who can think of little he'd like less than "getting intimate with Jesus".

Hepher (n.)
An elderly group member who asks the leader to repeat the reference that has just been read out four times.

Hermogenes (pl. n.)
Those individuals who have God so comfortably contained within a box that they are constantly bewildered by all the others who don't understand him.

Hezekiah (n.)
A book of the Bible that you spend ages looking for until you realize that it isn't a book of the Bible.

Hiddai (n.)
(Archaic) The piece of A4 paper that you place on the overhead projector so that you can add intrigue by unveiling one line of the acetate at a time.

Hittite (n.)
One towards whom your immediate and overwhelming pastoral instinct is to punch them really hard in the face.

Horonaim (n.)
A biblical word that even *kedorlaomers* can't pronounce.

Horonite (n.)
A youth sleepover in the church.

Hur (n.)
The minister's wife.

Hushah (n.)
The person that no one can identify who keeps making *shuas*.

Hushathite (n.)
The repeat offender who might be about to cause a *hushah* to become a *shunite* in a sudden outbreak of violence.

Hushim (v.)
What the music leader is dying to do to an *edom* but daren't because of a deep-seated fear of their equally loud parents.

I

Ichabod (n.)
One who knows your name, your spouse's name, and the names and ages of all of your children – even though, to your acute embarrassment, you weren't aware that they themselves existed until approximately thirteen seconds ago.

Idbash (v.)
To employ a succession of increasingly extreme measures in an attempt to deal with a *beeri* who is drinking considerably more than their fair share of the Communion wine.

Iddo (n.)
A particular kind of *lod* who, even after years in the church, still can't work out how Jesus was crucified only four months after he was born.

Illyricum (n.)
Any line in an otherwise acceptable song that you refuse to sing purely because it contains the word "wanna".

Isaiah (n.)
One who sings descant at the Carol Service.

Ishi (n.)
A measurement defined as the minimum appropriate distance between the hand of the one praying for healing and the body of the one being prayed for, when the body parts involved are of a sensitive nature.

Ishiah (n.)
A measurement equivalent to around thirteen *ishies* and defined as the minimum appropriate distance between the hand of the one praying for healing and the body of the one being prayed for, where the two involved are *hemen*.

Ishmael (n.)
One of those spineless and ineffective Christian men who makes you embarrassed to be a Christian. Or a man.

Italian (adj.)
The kind of wine you wish was in your Communion cup instead of the tasteless non-alcoholic substance that actually resides there.

Izziah (n.)
One who considers themselves to be a better Christian than everyone else, particularly when it comes to humility.

J

Jabal (n.)
The phenomenon where the sermon expands to fit whatever space remains for it.

Jabbok (n.)
The phenomenon where the sermon expands way beyond whatever space remains for it.

Jael (n.)
Despite every effort to lead them to God, this is the place to which it appears that most of the unchurched youth group are actually heading.

Jambres (pl. n.)
Those children's talks of which everyone remembers the illustration but no one has any idea what the point was.

Jamin (n.)
That which the church up the road's doughnuts have, that your cheap church biscuits don't.

Jarmuth (n.)
A seaside town that no one has ever heard of, yet which somehow becomes the location for the church weekend away before anyone discovers it's actually on the outskirts of Birmingham.

Javan (n.)
The utterly inconsequential computer programme that the operator blames for ruining "Carols by Candlelight" in order to disguise the fact that he dozed off halfway through "Christians Awake".

Jehonathan (n.)
A member of the congregation who is actually called Jehonathan due to a minor clerical error by a registrar who is a particular fan of obscure Levites.

Jehoshaphat (n.)
A youth worker in his thirties who speaks like a sixteen-year-old in a futile attempt to be "down with the kids".

Jemimah (n.)
The furtive but desperate sideways glance of a young child who has joined the others on stage for an action song, despite having never heard the song before.

Jeroboam (n.)
The allegedly small quantity of wine left over after Communion that the minister has to drink.

Jesher (n.)
One who stands up after an appeal, not because they want to respond, but because they are terribly worried that no one else will and they don't want the preacher to be disappointed.

Jeshua (n.)
Jehonathan's younger brother. Same registrar.

Jesse (n.)
A slang term for a man dressed in a cassock.

Jeuel (n.)
That part of the sermon which God has spoken to challenge you, and which you think is just what your friend needs to hear.

Jezebel (n.)
A lady who flagrantly disregards *mushi* etiquette by linking fingers with you.

Joppa (n.)
The ability to continue to turn your head from Bible to preacher and back, even though you are, to all intents and purposes, asleep.

Judas (n.)
One who finally gives up the ghost (Holy) and moves to the church up the road.

Junia (n.)
The intelligent young volunteer who is inadvertently outwitting you and thereby gently ruining your poorly thought out children's talk.

Justus (n.)
A prayer meeting of fewer than four people. It is impossible to begin praying at a justus until someone has quoted Matthew 18:20.

THE MOST UNRELIABLE BIBLE DICTIONARY, EVER!

Justus

"No really, honestly, thanks for asking, but we're all absolutely <u>fine</u>. I really, really only popped by to deliver the magazine."

Juttah (v.)

To start praying at the same time as someone else, and then both stop, and then move into the "go on", "no you go on" humble-a-thon.

K

Kabul (v.)
To say to someone in a crisis, "Let me know if there's anything I can do", only because you are certain they won't take you up on your offer.

Kadesh Barnea (n.)
A barely concealed look of utter disdain on the face of the minister. This is often reserved for the organist at the moment it is clear that they have completely taken over the proceedings with their incompetence.

Kadmiel (n.)
One who uses the mythical substance "felt led" as an excuse for having done whatever the heck they wanted.

Kamon (n.)
What everyone is dying to shout at the preacher during an *addon*.

Kanah (n.)
The insistent question that is eventually repeated enough times so as to become the launch point for a *kilmad*.

Kandake (n.)
A white-hot rage you experience the first time you realize that, despite your erudite and impassioned plea at the last church meeting, that thing is still happening.

Karkas (n.)
One who lies facedown during a prayer meeting. This is the only position with which you can trump a *beno* for humility, and is essentially a spiritual version of "Sleeping Lions".

Karshena (n.)
The only member of the youth outreach car-washing crew to actually wash some car.

Kedorlaomer (n.)
One who is always asked to read passages that are full of unpronounceable names.

Kenan (n.)
One who actually turns up to church on time.

Kenites (pl. n.)
That small pack of worried dogs milling about the door of a church blessed with a large collection of *bezers*.

Kibroth Hattaavah (n.)
An unremitting tantrum delivered by an apparently somewhat dissatisfied inmate of your crèche, which gives you genuine concerns that you are shortly going to have to consult the minister about how to perform an exorcism.

Kilmad (n.)
An uncontrolled parental outburst directed towards an errant child that ceases abruptly when the parent suddenly remembers they're in church.

Kish (n.)
A kiss suddenly planted on you by someone you really didn't expect to receive one from. And really didn't want to receive one from.

Kitlish (adj.)
Prone towards pretending to know the person talking to you much better than you actually do, especially if they are an *ichabod*.

Kos (n.)
The reason given by a new minister for changing something that they had no reason to change. This often helps greatly towards them being considered *abaddon*.

Kushaiah (n.)
The extremely young soprano in the choir who stands on their hassock when singing so that they can almost be seen by the congregation.

L

Laadah (n.)
One who sings slightly ahead of everyone else. This is usually done with such conviction that it is easier for the assembled musicians to try to catch the laadah up, than to keep to tempo.

Land of Nod (n.)
The place you are unintentionally residing whilst between a *beth dagon* and a *dagon*.

Lasea (n.)
One who uses "It's somewhere in the Bible" as an excuse to peddle some ridiculous theological idea that is in opposition to the rest of Scripture.

Lasha (v.)
What some people, despite Jesus' best efforts to educate them, still think we should do to a woman caught in adultery.

Lazarus (n.)
The previous minister who was universally disliked but is now considered to be better than the new one in every possible way.

Levites (pl. n.)
The numerous and increasingly more desperate attempts to get away from someone who continues to talk at you after the service, but to whom you are no longer listening because you have spotted someone else you need to catch.

Likhi (n.)
One who, on the way out of church, can't think of anything better to say to the preacher than that their sermon was "nice".

Linus (n.)
An old white crocheted tablecloth that is laid over the Communion elements and eventually whipped off with a flourish by the minister.

Lod (n.)
The least intelligent child in your Sunday School group, often a tightly fought contest.

Lo-Ruhamah (n.)
One who shamelessly shares extremely sensitive information about another, which is sometimes very nearly accurate, by offering it "for prayer".

Lud (n.)
The child brought by your *lod*, the only one to rise to the challenge of bringing a friend to church, who, to everyone's amazement, is comfortably less intelligent than the *lod* himself.

Ludites (pl. n.)
All the family members of the *lud*, which he inconsiderately brings along the following week.

Luke (v.)
To pretend to be joining in with an action song by pulling all the right facial expressions, while simultaneously ensuring that you don't actually do a single action.

M

Madmannah (n.)
The moment when a small "neutral" comment generates such an instantaneous and unprecedented torrent of incandescent rage that you are forced to conclude that, pastorally speaking, you are possibly not quite on the ball.

Madon (n.)
The clearly livid response from a church full of people, which the clueless carer of the small witless child who is currently damaging an expensive drum kit misreads as "amused and indulgent".

Magadan (adj.)
In complete agreement with the point the preacher just made. This is expressed by means of affirmative head movements and small humming noises.

Magog (adj.)
In complete disagreement with the point the preacher just made. This is expressed by means of wide eyes and an open mouth.

Matred (n.)
A feeling of murderous revenge against your tyrannical puritan mother which you quietly send back into the dark recesses of your mind because that isn't what Christians are supposed to feel.

Matri (n.)
The sudden feeling of worry during a marriage service that the whole thing is going to come to an abrupt end somewhere around the lawful impediment bit.

Medad (n.)
What a *gezer* calls God in another successful attempt to incur the wrath of those who are *urbanus*.

Melchizedek (n.)
One whose name appears on every church list despite the fact that no one has the slightest idea who they are.

Memukan (n.)
The art of remembering the insignificant prayer requests that the rest of the group have forgotten about.

Mene (adj.)
That which you are sure others think you are as you allow the offering to pass you by. This leads to an overwhelming desire to tell people around you that you give by direct debit and is often the first step towards becoming a *gadder*.

Mephibosheth (n.)
A sudden, spontaneous splutter at a church meeting that conveys two-parts horror at what is being proposed with one-part unutterable contempt for the proposer, but which is nonetheless the final thing the mephiboshether has to say on the matter.

Meremoth (n.)
One who tells you God has given them a picture for you of "an eagle overtaking a dove in front of a rainbow, both low-flying over a newly furrowed field with a river flowing through it, as the sun rises in the background; the eagle may or may not have had some broken chains in his claws, it was hard to see" and then leaves you trying to work out what the heck it's supposed to mean.

Mesopotamia (n.)
The large, untidy pile of acetates in the cupboard that no-one will throw away, even though not one of them has been used since the 90s.

THE MOST UNRELIABLE BIBLE DICTIONARY, EVER!

Mesopotamia

"Hello, Emergency Services? Search and Rescue, please."

Messiah (n.)
The collection of all kinds of useless rubbish in the balcony that no one has the time or the inclination to sort through and dispose of.

Micah (n.)
One who rushes around looking important whenever there is a problem with the sound, but who actually appears to be making no difference whatsoever.

Micaiah (n.)
The uniquely sized individual who stands at the pulpit to read and causes a kerfuffle as the *micah* rushes to the front to adjust the gooseneck.

Migdol (n.)
A toy that is old, dirty, and broken, and which has been sacrificially donated to the church for the crèche.

Mikloth (n.)
(Archaic) The stained white doily used to clean the rim of the *nimshi*.

Mikmash (n.)
A first attempt at preaching.

Milkah (n.)
One who, having been invited to share a two-minute piece of testimony in a tightly scheduled service, ends up taking up fifteen minutes by telling two other banal stories, recounting a slightly dubious joke, and then advertising some trivial secular cause to which they want people to give.

Miniamin (n.)
The preacher's closing prayer that is basically a shortened rehash of their sermon.

Minnith (n.)
This is the measurement used for the experienced length of a sermon and is intrinsically linked to the level of interest of the sermon concerned. Well-known preachers at Christian conferences always seem to be able to fit a fifty-minute sermon into fifteen minniths, whereas your own minister somehow manages to make a twenty-minute thought last for over forty-five minniths, which you'll never get back.

Mishmannah (n.)
The half-clap, half-dance that parents employ to embarrass their kids during a children's song.

Mispar (n.)
A line in a song that makes absolutely no sense to any reasonable-minded person and yet is still sung purposefully by all, for example "Lord make me a mountain", "I was like a goose on the loose", or anything by Ishmael in the 70s. Or the 80s.

Mithnite (n.)
The fabled and much spoken of evening service of countless years ago when apparently someone actually became a Christian.

Mizar (n.)
One who has a deep love of Jesus, but not quite as deep as their pockets.

Mordecai (n.)
The feeling of horror when you realize that the *milkah* has just got back up and is now brandishing a guitar.

Moses (pl. n.)
The affirmative humming noises that people feel obligated to make while someone else is praying.

Mount of Olives (n.)
The large quantity of food left over after the funeral of someone who clearly wasn't as popular as people thought.

Muppim (n.)
An adult who always shouts out the answers to the questions being asked of the children, and then throws as many people as possible their "How good am I?" look.

Mushi (n.)
The "share the love" moment when the service leader makes you hold hands with the people on either side of you for the closing prayer.

N

Naaman (n.)
One who resolutely, and rather loudly, continues to sing the old words to the updated version of their favourite hymn.

Naboth (n.)
An empty front row.

Naggai (n.)
A more commonly used name for the church secretary.

Nahum (n.)
One who is now mortally offended because they looked at you while *zeebing* and you didn't look at them.

Naphish (adj.)
(Of the face) Feigning a rueful fondness for babies while seeking to publicly bless a child that is trying to win its first screaming contest.

Nazirite (n.)
A hard of hearing Alpha guest who thinks he needs to commit his life to cheeses.

Nebuchadnezzar (n.)
A loud stomach rumble during a prayer meeting that requires you to explain that it wasn't what it sounded like. Nebuchadnezzars become particularly prevalent during periods of prayer and fasting.

Nehemiah (n.)
The belief held by many *uriahs* that they are safe because, not unlike a Dalek, the Holy Spirit can only move around on the ground floor.

Neiel (n.)
The only remaining member of the congregation who uses a hassock when praying.

Nergal (n.)
One who can always be counted on to burst into a dreary 70s chorus whenever there is a moment of quiet during a prayer meeting.

Nicolaitans (pl. n.)
Those who are the most consistently regular attendees of the whole church in that they turn up once a year, every year, on Christmas Day.

Nimrah (n.)
A shuffling noise made during small group prayer that is designed to let everyone know that the prayer time has come to an end.

Nimrim (v.)
(Archaic) To turn the *nimshi* round and drink from the other side even though the *mikloth* was used very diligently after the previous person.

THE MOST UNRELIABLE BIBLE DICTIONARY, EVER!

Neiel

"Bernard's our last hope – once he goes, that's it – EVICTION!"

Nimrod (n.)
One who prays first and covers every request, leaving the rest of the group desperately struggling to find something they can talk to God about.

Nimshi (n.)
The large silver cup that due to reasons of environmental health can no longer be used for the wine, yet due to reasons of tradition is still brought out and waved around at the appropriate moment.

Noadiah (n.)
Any complicated theological word in a sermon that only one person in the building understands, occasionally the preacher.

Noah (n.)
A highly gifted individual who continually turns down every ministry opportunity offered to them.

Nobah (n.)
Any church social event at which alcohol is strictly prohibited, and therefore one that those from outside of the church do their level best to avoid along with most of the church.

O

Obadiah (n.)
The flash of panic in a minister's mind when having whimsically imagined the pews filled with crash test dummies, the realization hits that life would be a lot easier if they were.

Og (v.)
To make an audible sound of disappointment during the sermon when after forty *minniths* the preacher says, "We'll look at this in more detail later".

Ohel (n.)
An involuntary noise uttered by a minister when confronted with a group of elderly, but not quite demented, ladies who are seriously proposing themselves as a worship-singing ensemble.

Omar (n.)

A young mum who remains in the crèche with her baby, not out of any desire to help, but because the gurgling that comes out of her baby's mouth will probably make more sense than anything that comes out of the mouth of today's preacher.

Ono (n.)

One who is almost always the first up to the front when the opportunity arises for testimony to be brought. Ironically, if you could choose to ban just one individual from coming up at that point, it would be this one.

P

Padon (n.)
The vaguely interesting piece of information that adds precisely nothing to the message but which the preacher includes anyway because they spent ages researching it.

Pamphylia (n.)
A condition which forces the sufferer to politely accept any religious leaflet offered at their door, even if they are certain it will be heretical. Sufferers must then rush immediately to the bin to dispose of it before it contaminates anything.

Pass of Adummim (n.)
The contrived attempt to manoeuvre the Communion elements from one end of the row to the other without allowing the single heathen in the middle to get hold of any.

Pau (n.)
The popping noise that a cheap microphone makes every time the preacher says a word beginning with "P". It is perhaps possible, but probably pretty painstaking, to prepare a preach that prohibits "P" words.

Pekah (n.)
One who complains about anything and everything but never actually does anything about anything.

Peor (n.)
A man who always seems to go out to the toilet during the sermon.

Persis (n.)
The mysterious individual who secretly smuggles quiche into every single Christian buffet. Anywhere. Ever.

Pharaoh (n.)
Something that is in a constant state of change, for example, the mood of the organist, the tempo of the drummer, and the hairstyle of the youth worker (cf. *samos*).

Pharisees (pl. n.)
Those Christians that you have decided are judgmental.

P

Pharpar (n.)
One who is sitting between a *haggite* and a *baalah*, and is therefore greatly relieved to have just been deafened by a *bezer*.

Philistine (n.)
One who responds to a *kabuller* by flagrantly taking them up on their offer.

Phrygia (n.)
A condition that, for reasons of conscience, renders one utterly incapable of throwing the *mount of olives* into a bin. It is instead left to loiter in the church fridge, where it remains until the day it can make its own way out.

Pilate (v.)
To carefully position buffet food in a way that enables you to heap the maximum possible amount on your small paper plate. You can be certain you have pilated if a) some of the food falls off as you walk to a chair and b) you end up totally full and having to force down a small triangular egg sandwich, a greasy chicken leg, and a large slice of dry pork pie.

Pinon (v.)
To blame someone for something that you are certain wasn't their fault, purely because you know them to be so graceful that they'll take it without complaint and apologize profusely.

Pishon (n.)
A completely innocuous biblical word that a seven-year-old has just so spectacularly mispronounced that the members of the congregation who aren't mortally offended are desperately fighting for their next breath.

Pool of Siloam (n.)
The not insignificant body of water that has formed on the floor around a *bathsheba*.

Potiphar (v.)
To cause unnecessary accidents by positioning the mums and tots group a long way from the toilets.

Priscilla and Aquila (ns.)
A recently engaged couple who have suddenly, and for no apparent reason, become regular attendees of your beautiful old church, with its extensive grounds set in picturesque countryside.

Puah (n.)
A *peor* or *beth peor* who only reappears when the coffee is being served.

Pudens (pl. n.)
The shufflings and murmurings in the pews that let you know that someone nearby has broken wind and the results are headed your way.

Pul (v.)
What a *geder* is secretly hoping he'll be able to do, however unlikely it may be.

Punon (n.)
A minister who, often against their own professional interest, can't resist a good joke. Or a joke.

Q

Queen Vashti (n.)
An elderly lady who activates the church's emergency prayer chain late one evening because her budgie, Cyril, "isn't himself".

Quirinius (n.)
The mental calculus required to work out how large a piece you can tear from the Communion loaf without looking greedy and without leaving the last few participants with holy crumbs.

R

Rabbith (n.)
A small group prayer meeting at which the attendees spend 90 per cent of the time discussing what to pray for, and 5 per cent bemoaning the fact that they haven't started praying yet.

Rakkon (n.)
The satisfying assuaging of guilt that coincides with you putting your ten-pound lottery win in the offering.

Ramah (n.)
One whose only evangelism technique involves asking anyone and everyone whether they are "washed in the blood of the Lamb".

Reelaiah (n.)
One who sits back and lets others do the job that God has called them to do, and then complains when it isn't done properly.

Rekem (n.)
The attempt by a *hermogene* to comfort someone who is going through horrific hardship by telling them how simply it can all be explained and how much better they will feel if they just accept that.

Reuel (n.)
The obligation one feels to take up the "receive position" when being prayed for. This involves standing with both hands held palms up at waist height and is designed to convince God that you are ready for anything.

Reumah (n.)
Something you should never believe, however convincing it may sound, and however much you might want to.

Ribai (n.)
The food that you wish was on the table at the buffet lunch instead of the usual quiche.

Romamti-Ezer (n.)
One who believes Jesus is their boyfriend. Sometimes female.

Rufus (v.)
What your church's latest financial appeal is designed to do. Also the reason for the large drawing of a nearly empty thermometer stuck on the front of the church.

S

Sadducees (pl. n.)
Those whose joy is so deep that you would need to send in a team of extreme potholers to have any chance of locating it.

Salmon (n.)
The really nice, expensive food that you only ever get after an induction service, and which is only there to impress the new minister.

Samaria (n.)
A mental condition that forces you to sit in the same part of the church every week. The area you chose to put yourself that very first day, becomes the only area you ever head for from then on, no matter what. A move of more than four seats in any direction from your original position simply leaves you discombobulated and utterly unable to hear from God.

Samaritan (n.)
That non-Christian friend of yours who rather frustratingly behaves much more like a Christian than any of the Christians you know.

Samos (n.)
Something that is unchangeable, for example God, the position of the Communion table, and the intractability of the church secretary (cf. *pharaoh*).

Sardis (n.)
A church that, once you get inside, is much bigger than you thought.

Seled (n.)
Something healthy that you'll never find on the plate of a *colossae* as it takes up valuable space that is required for things made out of pastry.

Sephar (n.)
One who always sits on the back row.

Shalmaneser (n.)
Someone who whispers in tongues whenever God is so much as mentioned in passing.

THE MOST UNRELIABLE BIBLE DICTIONARY, EVER!

Sardis

St Saviour's was having difficulty raising funds for a mobility access facility.

Shamgar (v.)
To choose an obscure Bible translation for one of your vital supporting verses because it is the only version in which that verse sounds like it is making the point you need it to make.

Shammah (n.)
One who loves their church passionately, then takes a Sunday off when it's their birthday. Or their spouse's birthday. Or any of their kids' birthdays. Or the dog's.

Shamsherai (n.)
The vocal mayhem caused by songwriters who think it would be pleasing and authentic to have a line in Hebrew.

Sharezer (n.)
One who, when you politely ask them how they are, has the audacity to waste ten minutes of your life telling you.

Sheshbazzar (n.)
One who is a regular and generous donator of second-hand equipment to the church, solely because it is considerably closer than the refuse tip. Often the supplier of *migdols*.

Shiloah (n.)
A member of a *titus* who arrives late and has to sit on the floor.

Shinar (n.)
That which is currently being sported by an *adoraim* after he not so cleverly tried the same trick at his local pub.

Shua (n.)
The sudden sound made during a service which is designed to silence someone who is making a noise. This is the sound employed with great success by *hushahs* and with no effect by *shunites*.

Shulammite (n.)
One who accidentally produces a *nimrah* while fidgeting, thereby bringing the prayer time to a premature end and offending all those who didn't have their request prayed for.

Shunammite (n.)
The elderly individual who clearly heard your *tychicus* because they are now looking at you with a mixture of shock and disappointment in their eyes.

Shunite (n.)
A *hushah* whose identity has been exposed and who has therefore lost whatever mysterious power they held that caused their *shuas* to be so effective in the first place.

Sinites (pl. n.)
Those challenging individuals who respond diligently at every possible public opportunity, yet never seem to change in the slightest.

Sitnah (n.)
One who uses every item at their disposal, and some things that are not, to save an entire row of seats for others who may or may not turn up. Sometimes *solomons* do this to prevent anyone sitting near them.

Smyrna (n.)
A condition where the sufferer secretly holds the view that the saints who wrote the Psalms were nothing but a bunch of whiners.

Sodom and Gomorrah (ns.)
The two most appallingly behaved youngsters in Sunday School who, by a remarkable coincidence, both happen to be children of the minister.

Solomon (n.)
That person who always leaves immediately after the service without speaking to anyone, then after a year complains that they don't feel part of the church.

Spain (n.)
That quiet, steely certainty that someone should do something about it. But obviously not you.

Stachys (pl. n.)
The ugly wax marks that need to be scraped off the Communion table after Advent.

Stoic (n.)
One of those slightly old-fashioned churches for whom a PowerPoint is a mains socket for the vacuum cleaner.

Syntyche (n.)
A minor, insignificant sin that you're certain you've got away with because only someone omniscient could possibly know about it.

Syracuse (v.)
To be great at pointing out other people's sin and utterly unable to see your own, especially when it's exactly the same sin.

T

Tabor (n.)
The apparent goal of today's preacher.

Tadmor (n.)
That which the worship leader always seems to want of themselves in the fold-back monitor.

Tarshish (adj.)
(Of the face) Failing to remain *naphish* and trying desperately hard to not go into a *kadesh barnea*.

Tekel (v.)
To attempt to remove a sweet from its packaging without anyone noticing. This isn't so much because you are worried what people will think, but because you are worried they will want one.

Telem (v.)
What preachers think they need to do.

Terah (n.)
The look of long-haul panic in a pentecostally oriented preacher's eyes when their shout of "Can I get an 'Amen'?" appears to be being answered by a resounding "No".

Tertius (adj.)
A tertius sermon point is one that is so obviously contrived that you can be certain it only exists in order to reach the required number of three.

Tidal (adj.)
Of the baptistry when a *colossae* is being baptized.

Tishbite (v.)
To wait at a buffet lunch until everyone else has their food so that you can *pilate* without feeling guilty.

Titus (n.)
A home group or youth group that meets in a room that is far too small for them.

Tob (n.)
One small, solitary, red-stained Communion glass left overlooked on the floor. This is always found immediately after the sink has been emptied of washing-up water.

Tobijah (n.)
The tiny glass container in which the extra virgin anointing oil resides.

Traconitis (n.)
A suddenly hoarse voice that coincidentally overcomes a *kedorlaomer* at the very moment they get to a *horonaim*.

Tryphena (n.)
The pained expression on the face of the worship leader that makes you certain they are either desperately in need of prayer ministry or the toilet.

Tychicus (n.)
The muttered swear word you let out during a particularly frustrating church meeting, which is usually followed by a quick glance round to check that no one heard.

Tyrannus (n.)
One who has absolutely no authority but wields it all regardless.

THE MOST UNRELIABLE BIBLE DICTIONARY, EVER!

Tyrannus

Creche duty was a testing time.

U

Ummah (n.)
One who emits a tuneless murmuring noise when trying to sing along to a hymn they don't know.

Ur (n.)
Response from a house group leader when asked a question about an obscure passage in Revelation. Or, in fact, any passage in Revelation. Or the Old Testament.

Urbanus (adj.)
Resolutely refined and polite when speaking to God. In other words, refusing to refer to him in any other way than the old-school "Thee" and "Thou".

Uriah (n.)
One who always sits in the balcony.

Uzal (n.)
That kind of church toilet paper that is more suited to sanding the walls than wiping sensitive Christian bottoms.

Uzzah (n.)
The uzzah is the precise instant somewhere between the last word of the verse and the first of the chorus at which all hands are simultaneously raised in spontaneous worship.

Uzzi (n.)
What you wish you had at your disposal during a particularly lengthy *addon*.

Uzziah (n.)
A group of individuals who have unintentionally become *isaiahs*, and tortuously bad ones, because the *isaiah* at the front is singing so loudly that they can no longer pick out the regular melody.

V

Vaniah (n.)
Who you end up having to call to rescue the youth trip after the minibus fails to start again.

Vophsi (n.)
One who perennially complains about church not finishing on time but who is nonetheless currently basking in the joy of an apparently eternal Spring Harvest session.

THE MOST UNRELIABLE BIBLE DICTIONARY, EVER!

Vaniah

"Sorry mate, I'm not licensed to carry more than 12 – can't you call someone local for the minister's kids?"

Z

Zabad (n.)
The moment of extreme awkwardness that occurs when two *hemen* are sitting next to each other and a *mushi* is announced.

Zalaph (n.)
A desperate but ultimately unsuccessful bid not to burst into giggles at the inadvertent but obvious innuendo that just did a much better job of grabbing everyone's attention than the rest of the sermon.

Zamzummites (pl. n.)
The extremely unconvincing coughing noises that inevitably follow on from a *zalaph*.

Zaphenath-Paneah (n.)
An attempt to force the gift of tongues.

Zebedee (n.)
One who used to love the church but then experienced the wonder of Spring Harvest for the first time and came back a *pekah*.

Zeeb (v.)
To look around at each other when saying the grace together.

Zephon (n.)
A feeling of smug disapproval that washes over you when someone's mobile phone rings during a service.

Zephonite (n.)
One who deliberately rings someone else's mobile phone during the service in order to feel *zephon*.

Zerubabbel (n.)
The realization after five minutes waiting for an interpretation that the individual concerned isn't in fact speaking in tongues but has just come to the prayer meeting directly from the dentist.

Ziklag (n.)
A mysterious sensation in the stomach that could be a move of the Spirit or of the cheese you ate the night before.

Ziph (n.)
A measure of time equal to 0.027 seconds (or about half that in the case of an *amok*). This is the precise amount of time it takes for a child to volunteer for a children's talk following any use of the word "chocolate".

Ziv (v.)
To say you'll pray for someone with all good intentions but then completely forget.

Zophar (n.)
One of those testimonies where life is fantastic right up to the point they became a Christian.

Zuriel (n.)
The new church plant up the road that your church is populating by sacrificially sending them four *cretans*, the *lod* and the *ludites*, a *kadmiel*, a couple of *muppims*, three *pekahs*, a *milkah*, and an entire homegroup of *sadducees*. Oh, and congratulations, you're the minister.

THE MOST UNRELIABLE BIBLE DICTIONARY, EVER!

Ziph

"Are there any Fair Trade Chocolates?"

Bible References

A

Abaddon	Revelation 9:11
Abdi	Ezra 10:26
Abel	Genesis 4:2
Abel Maim	2 Chronicles 16:4
Abishag	1 Kings 1:3
Achaicus	1 Corinthians 16:17
Achish	1 Samuel 21:10
Addon	Ezra 2:59
Adin	Ezra 8:6
Adoraim	2 Chronicles 11:9
Agag	1 Samuel 15:8
Agrippa	Acts 25:13
Ahikam	2 Kings 22:12
Ahira	Numbers 1:15
Ahuzzath	Genesis 26:26
Ai	Joshua 7:2
Aiah	2 Samuel 21:8
Akbor	2 Kings 22:12
Amaziah	2 Kings 14:1
Amok	Nehemiah 12:7
Amorite	Genesis 14:13
Anem	1 Chronicles 6:73
Ararat	Isaiah 37:38
Arimathea	Matthew 27:57
Armageddon	Revelation 16:16
Arumah	Judges 9:41
Attai	1 Chronicles 2:35
Azbuk	Nehemiah 3:16

B

Baal	Judges 2:13
Baal Gad	Joshua 11:17
Baal Meon	Ezekiel 25:9
Baal Zephon	Exodus 14:2
Baalah	Joshua 15:9
Baanah	2 Samuel 4:2
Babylon	1 Peter 5:13
Bakbuk	Ezra 2:51
Bamah	Ezekiel 20:29
Barabbas	Mark 15:7
Bathsheba	2 Samuel 11:3
Beeri	Hosea 1:1
Beno	1 Chronicles 24:26
Beri	1 Chronicles 7:36
Besor	1 Samuel 30:9
Beth Dagon	Joshua 15:41
Beth Nimrah	Numbers 32:36
Beth Peor	Deuteronomy 3:29
Betonim	Joshua 13:26
Bezer	2 Peter 2:15
Blastus	Acts 12:20
Bokim	Judges 2:1
Bul	1 Kings 6:38
Buzi	Ezekiel 1:3
Byblos	Psalm 83:7

C

Caesar	Matthew 22:17
Cain	Jude 1:11
Carchemish	Jeremiah 46:2
Castor and Pollux	Acts 28:11
Chuza	Luke 8:3

Clement	Philippians 4:3
Colossae	Colossians 1:2
Cretans	Titus 1:12
Crispus	Acts 18:8
Cush	Nahum 3:9
Cushi	Zephaniah 1:1

D

Dagon	Judges 16:23
Dalmatia	2 Timothy 4:10
Darkon	Nehemiah 7:58
Dedan	Genesis 25:3
Desert of Zin	Deuteronomy 32:51
Deuel	Numbers 7:42
Diblaim	Hosea 1:3
Dibon Gad	Numbers 33:45
Dishan	Genesis 36:21
Dodo	Judges 10:1
Dor	1 Chronicles 7:29
Dorcas	Acts 9:36

E

Edom	Malachi 1:4
Eldaah	Genesis 25:4
Eli	1 Samuel 3:1
Eltekon	Joshua 15:59
Esau	Genesis 25:25
Eutychus	Acts 20:9

F

Felix	Acts 24:2
Festus	Acts 25:1
Fortunatus	1 Corinthians 16:17

THE MOST UNRELIABLE BIBLE DICTIONARY, EVER!

G

Gaash	2 Samuel 23:30
Gad	Genesis 30:11
Gadarenes	Matthew 8:28
Gaius	3 John 1:1
Garmite	1 Chronicles 4:19
Gath Hepher	2 Kings 14:25
Geber	1 Kings 4:19
Geder	Joshua 12:13
Gerasenes	Luke 8:26
Gether	Genesis 10:23
Gezer	2 Samuel 5:25
Gideon	Judges 6:11
Gittites	2 Samuel 15:18
Gob	2 Samuel 21:18
Gog	Ezekiel 38:2
Goshen	Exodus 9:26
Gudgodah	Deuteronomy 10:7
Guni	1 Chronicles 5:15
Gur Baal	2 Chronicles 26:7

H

Habakkuk	Habakkuk 1:1
Habazziniah	Jeremiah 35:3
Hadoram	1 Chronicles 18:10
Haggai	Haggai 1:1
Haggite	Numbers 26:15
Hallelujah	Revelation 19:1
Ham	Genesis 5:32
Hamonah	Ezekiel 39:16
Hannathon	Joshua 19:14
Harhur	Ezra 2:51
Harim	Nehemiah 3:11

Hasadiah	1 Chronicles 3:20
Hatita	Ezra 2:42
Havilah	1 Samuel 15:7
Hazaiah	Nehemiah 11:5
Hazzelelponi	1 Chronicles 4:3
Hebrews	Philippians 3:5
Helam	2 Samuel 10:16
Heldai	Zechariah 6:10
Helek	Joshua 17:2
Heman	1 Chronicles 2:6
Hepher	Joshua 17:3
Hermogenes	2 Timothy 1:15
Hezekiah	2 Kings 18:1
Hiddai	2 Samuel 23:30
Hittite	Joshua 1:4
Horonaim	Isaiah 15:5
Horonite	Nehemiah 2:10
Hur	Exodus 17:10
Hushah	1 Chronicles 4:4
Hushathite	2 Samuel 21:18
Hushim	1 Chronicles 8:8

I

Ichabod	1 Samuel 4:21
Idbash	1 Chronicles 4:3
Iddo	Zechariah 1:1
Illyricum	Romans 15:19
Isaiah	Isaiah 1:1
Ishi	1 Chronicles 2:31
Ishiah	1 Chronicles 7:3
Ishmael	Genesis 16:11
Italian	Acts 10:1
Izziah	Ezra 10:25

J

Jabal	Genesis 4:20
Jabbok	Genesis 32:22
Jael	Judges 4:17
Jambres	2 Timothy 3:8
Jamin	Nehemiah 8:7
Jarmuth	Nehemiah 11:29
Javan	1 Chronicles 1:5
Jehonathan	2 Chronicles 17:8
Jehoshaphat	Joel 3:2
Jemimah	Job 42:14
Jeroboam	Amos 1:1
Jesher	1 Chronicles 2:18
Jeshua	1 Chronicles 24:11
Jesse	Ruth 4:17
Jeuel	Ezra 8:13
Jezebel	Revelation 2:20
Joppa	Jonah 1:3
Judas	Matthew 26:16
Junia	Romans 16:7
Justus	Colossians 4:11
Juttah	Joshua 15:55

K

Kabul	1 Kings 9:13
Kadesh Barnea	Deuteronomy 1:19
Kadmiel	Ezra 3:9
Kamon	Judges 10:5
Kanah	Joshua 19:28
Kandake	Acts 8:27
Karkas	Esther 1:10
Karshena	Esther 1:14
Kedorlaomer	Genesis 14:1

Kenan	Luke 3:37
Kenites	Numbers 24:21
Kibroth Hattaavah	Deuteronomy 9:22
Kilmad	Ezekiel 27:23
Kish	Acts 13:21
Kitlish	Joshua 15:40
Kos	Acts 21:1
Kushaiah	1 Chronicles 15:17

L

Laadah	1 Chronicles 4:21
Land of Nod	Genesis 4:16
Lasea	Acts 27:8
Lasha	Genesis 10:19
Lazarus	John 11:1
Levites	Leviticus 25:33
Likhi	1 Chronicles 7:19
Linus	2 Timothy 4:21
Lod	1 Chronicles 8:12
Lo-Ruhamah	Hosea 1:6
Lud	1 Chronicles 1:17
Ludites	Genesis 10:13
Luke	Philemon 1:24

M

Madmannah	1 Chronicles 2:49
Madon	Joshua 11:1
Magadan	Matthew 15:39
Magog	Ezekiel 39:6
Matred	Genesis 36:39
Matri	1 Samuel 10:21
Medad	Numbers 11:26
Melchizedek	Hebrews 5:6

THE MOST UNRELIABLE BIBLE DICTIONARY, EVER!

Memukan	Esther 1:14
Mene	Daniel 5:26
Mephibosheth	2 Samuel 9:6
Meremoth	Ezra 8:33
Mesopotamia	Acts 7:2
Messiah	Matthew 1:1
Micah	Micah 1:1
Micaiah	2 Chronicles 17:7
Migdol	Numbers 33:7
Mikloth	1 Chronicles 8:32
Mikmash	Isaiah 10:28
Milkah	Numbers 36:11
Miniamin	2 Chronicles 31:15
Minnith	Ezekiel 27:17
Mishmannah	1 Chronicles 12:10
Mispar	Ezra 2:2
Mithnite	1 Chronicles 11:43
Mizar	Psalm 42:6
Mordecai	Esther 2:5
Moses	Exodus 2:10
Mount of Olives	John 8:1
Muppim	Genesis 46:21
Mushi	Exodus 6:19

N

Naaman	2 Kings 5:1
Naboth	1 Kings 21:1
Naggai	Luke 3:25
Nahum	Nahum 1:1
Naphish	1 Chronicles 1:31
Nazirite	Numbers 6:2
Nebuchadnezzar	2 Kings 24:1
Nehemiah	Nehemiah 1:1
Neiel	Joshua 19:27

Nergal	2 Kings 17:30
Nicolaitans	Revelation 2:6
Nimrah	Numbers 32:3
Nimrim	Isaiah 15:6
Nimrod	Micah 5:6
Nimshi	1 Kings 19:16
Noadiah	Nehemiah 6:14
Noah	Genesis 5:29
Nobah	Numbers 32:42

O

Obadiah	Obadiah 1:1
Og	Deuteronomy 1:4
Ohel	1 Chronicles 3:20
Omar	Genesis 36:11
Ono	Nehemiah 6:2

P

Padon	Ezra 2:44
Pamphylia	Acts 2:10
Pass of Adummim	Joshua 15:7
Pau	Genesis 36:39
Pekah	2 Kings 15:25
Peor	Numbers 23:28
Persis	Romans 16:12
Pharaoh	Genesis 46:33
Pharisees	Matthew 3:7
Pharpar	2 Kings 5:12
Philistine	1 Samuel 17:8
Phrygia	Acts 18:23
Pilate	Luke 23:1
Pinon	Genesis 36:41
Pishon	Genesis 2:11

Pool of Siloam	John 9:7
Potiphar	Genesis 37:36
Priscilla and Aquila	Romans 16:3
Puah	Exodus 1:15
Pudens	2 Timothy 4:21
Pul	2 Kings 15:19
Punon	Numbers 33:42

Q

Queen Vashti	Esther 1:9
Quirinius	Luke 2:2

R

Rabbith	Joshua 19:20
Rakkon	Joshua 19:46
Ramah	Hosea 5:8
Reelaiah	Ezra 2:2
Rekem	Numbers 31:8
Reuel	Exodus 2:18
Reumah	Genesis 22:24
Ribai	2 Samuel 23:29
Romamti-Ezer	1 Chronicles 25:4
Rufus	Romans 16:13

S

Sadducees	Mark 12:18
Salmon	Ruth 4:20
Samaria	Luke 17:11
Samaritan	Luke 10:33
Samos	Acts 20:15
Sardis	Revelation 3:1
Seled	1 Chronicles 2:30
Sephar	Genesis 10:30

Shalmaneser	2 Kings 17:3
Shamgar	Judges 3:31
Shammah	2 Samuel 23:11
Shamsherai	1 Chronicles 8:26
Sharezer	Zechariah 7:2
Sheshbazzar	Ezra 1:8
Shiloah	Isaiah 8:6
Shinar	Genesis 11:2
Shua	Genesis 38:2
Shulammite	Song of Songs 6:13
Shunammite	1 Kings 1:3
Shunite	Numbers 26:15
Sinites	Genesis 10:17
Sitnah	Genesis 26:21
Smyrna	Revelation 2:8
Sodom and Gomorrah	Genesis 18:20
Solomon	Proverbs 1:1
Spain	Romans 15:24
Stachys	Romans 16:9
Stoic	Acts 17:18
Syntyche	Philippians 4:2
Syracuse	Acts 28:12

T

Tabor	Hosea 5:1
Tadmor	2 Chronicles 8:4
Tarshish	Jonah 1:3
Tekel	Daniel 5:27
Telem	Ezra 10:24
Terah	Genesis 11:24
Tertius	Romans 16:22
Tidal	Genesis 14:1
Tishbite	1 Kings 17:1
Titus	Titus 1:4

Tob	Judges 11:3
Tobijah	Zechariah 6:10
Traconitis	Luke 3:1
Tryphena	Romans 16:12
Tychicus	Ephesians 6:21
Tyrannus	Acts 19:9

U

Ummah	Joshua 19:30
Ur	Genesis 11:28
Urbanus	Romans 16:9
Uriah	2 Samuel 11:3
Uzal	1 Chronicles 1:21
Uzzah	2 Samuel 6:3
Uzzi	Ezra 7:4
Uzziah	Amos 1:1

V

Vaniah	Ezra 10:36
Vophsi	Numbers 13:14

Z

Zabad	1 Chronicles 2:36
Zalaph	Nehemiah 3:30
Zamzummites	Deuteronomy 2:20
Zaphenath-Paneah	Genesis 41:45
Zebedee	Mark 1:19
Zeeb	Judges 7:25
Zephon	Genesis 46:16
Zephonite	Numbers 26:15
Zerubabbel	Luke 3:27
Ziklag	1 Samuel 27:6
Ziph	Joshua 15:24

Ziv	1 Kings 6:1
Zophar	Job 2:11
Zuriel	Numbers 3:35